NARRATIVE POEMS

CHILDREN'S LIBRARY

BY YVONNE PEARSON

ILLUSTRATED BY KATHLEEN PETELINSEK

Published by The Child's World®
1980 Lookout Drive · Mankato, MN 56003-1705
800-599-READ · www.childsworld.com

ACKNOWLEDGMENTS
The Child's World®: Mary Berendes, Publishing Director
Red Line Editorial: Editorial direction
The Design Lab: Design and production

Photographs ©: Jorge Salcedo/Thinkstock, 6; iStock/
Thinkstock, 10; Fuse/Thinkstock, 13

ISBN 9781631436994
LCCN 2014945308

Printed in the United States of America
Mankato, MN
November, 2014
PA02240

About the Author

Yvonne Pearson is a poet and a social worker. She has published many poems and won contests. She writes essays and books, too. She lives in Minneapolis, Minnesota. She also lives in California near her grandchildren part of each year. Her Web site is *www.yvonnepearson.com*.

About the Illustrator

Kathleen Petelinsek is a graphic designer and illustrator. She has been designing and illustrating books for children for 20 years. She lives in Minnesota with her husband, two dogs, a cat, and three fancy chickens.

TABLE OF CONTENTS

What Is a Poem?

"Ring around the rosie, a pocket full of posies." Have you said this on the playground? Did you know you were reciting a poem? Have you ever said "Eenie meenie miney moe"? You were saying a poem!

Poems have been part of people's lives for thousands of years. Poetry helps people remember things they care about. It can also remind readers of certain emotions. Poetry can even teach readers to look at something in a whole new way.

Poetry can be about anything. It can describe things you see. But it can also be about things you imagine.

Poetry usually says a lot with a few words. A poem is often written in lines instead of sentences. A line can be very long. Or it can be as short as one or two words! Poets usually try to use words in ways that are pleasing to listen to. They often use descriptive words. Poets try to write poems that help readers picture what the poem is about.

WHAT IS A NARRATIVE POEM?

A narrative poem tells a story. In fact, that's the only rule of narrative poetry! Like any story, narrative poetry has a beginning, middle, and end. A narrative poem has a **plot**. This is made up of the events that happen in a story. It has a setting. This is where the story takes place. Narrative poems have **characters**. These are the people or animals that appear in a story.

"Paul Revere's Ride" is a famous narrative poem by Henry Wadsworth Longfellow. It is about the time when America fought for independence from Great Britain. The poem tells the story of Paul Revere, who goes on a brave horseback ride to warn colonists that British soldiers are coming.

Narrative poems often start out with a description of the setting and the main character.

Many narrative poems are fiction. This means they are made-up stories. Some narrative poems are nonfiction. These are true stories.

People have used narrative poetry to tell stories for thousands of years. In ancient times, people used narrative poems to tell their history. Books were not yet common. Groups listened to poems.

People still read and listen to narrative poems. Perhaps you have heard of "Casey at the Bat" by Ernest Thayer. It is an exciting narrative poem about baseball. "The Walrus and the Carpenter" is a silly poem written by Lewis Carroll. It is about a walrus and a carpenter who go for a walk on the beach. They trick some oysters into walking with them. Then they eat the oysters!

Carlos and His Dog

Young Carlos was a little boy.
He just turned ten years old.
He lived in a house beside a lake
and when it was no longer cold
he took his dog out for a walk
in the forest dark and deep.
He hoped to see if bears had left
their dens at last to eat.
But the dog didn't know that bears,
like boys and girls, of course,
get cranky when they're hungry
and growl and snarl and worse.
The dog got excited and jumped right up
to lick a big bear's nose.
The bear swiped the dog with his paw.
The dog—he cried and rose.

He flew ten feet in the air,
landing on the ground below.
Carlos and his dog turned and ran
before the bear struck another blow.
Carlos said to his dog that day,
"If you want to walk with me,
don't get up in a big bear's face."
The little dog said, "I agree."

?
Who are the characters in this poem?
How would you describe the setting?

CHAPTER TWO

2

Rhyme and Rhythm

Poets use many different tools when they write poems. The tools help make a poem's words sound interesting or pleasing. Some tools make narrative poetry different from regular stories.

You can make a list of words before you even write a poem. Then use these words in your poem!

Rhyme is a tool poets often use in narrative poetry. Words that rhyme have the same ending sounds. *Mad* and *sad* rhyme. So do *kitten* and *mitten*. Rhymes make poems easier to memorize. Ancient narrative poems shared a lot of information and history. These poems could be very long. Rhyme helped the people reciting a poem remember it.

WHAT IS RHYTHM?

Rhythm also makes a poem easier to remember. Most narrative poems use rhythm. Rhythm is the pattern of sounds in a poem. All words are broken up into syllables. These are the parts that make up a word. *Hal-lo-ween* has three syllables. *Hand-some* has two. *Ice* just has one syllable.

Rhythm makes some poems sound like music.
Many poems are even turned into songs.

Some syllables are stressed. This means they are spoken a little bit louder than other syllables. Unstressed syllables are spoken more softly. The first syllable is stressed in *RAD-ish*. The second syllable is stressed in *in-DEED*. The arrangement of stressed and unstressed syllables creates a poem's rhythm.

A poem's rhythm pattern is known as meter. Meter is measured in feet. In poetry, each foot has a certain number of stressed and unstressed syllables. For example *da-DUM* is one foot. Then, *da-DUM da-DUM* is two feet. The line "The kitten chased my dog away" has four feet.

foot 1	**foot 2**	**foot 3**	**foot 4**
The KIT-	ten CHASED	my DOG	aWAY.

Meters and feet can be complicated. But having a certain number of feet is not the most important thing about poetry. Having fun with poems is most important!

The Kitten and the Puppy Dog

The kitten and the puppy dog
had always been the best of friends.
They chased each other all day long
Played hide and seek around the bend.
One day they ran so fast, so fast
They got into a tangled pose.
The puppy found he had cat ears
And kitten had the puppy's nose.

?

How many feet are there in each line of this poem?

Epics and Ballads

Narrative poetry does not have many rules. But there are many ways to write a narrative poem. Poets can write many different forms of narrative poetry. Epic poems and ballads are two of the most well-known forms.

EPIC POEMS

Epic poems are serious poems. They feature heroes and heroines. The heroes of epic poems often go on difficult journeys. They may have to perform a very hard task.

Epic poems often have gods or magic in them. They can be very long. Some epic poems are as long as a book. The *Iliad* and the *Odyssey* are two famous epic poems. An ancient Greek poet named Homer wrote them more than 2,000 years ago. Both poems are about a war. A more modern epic poem is *The Song of Hiawatha* by Henry Wadsworth Longfellow. That poem is less than two hundred years old. It tells the story of a Native American man named Hiawatha.

BALLADS

Ballads are another common form of narrative poetry. They are much shorter than epics. They often tell dramatic stories. They might discuss historical events, legends, or love. Ballads are often sung instead of read. Because they are sung, ballads usually use rhythm and rhyme.

Most ballads are broken into groups of lines called **stanzas**. Each stanza is usually four lines long. The second and fourth lines of each stanza rhyme.

On the next page is a ballad about Rosa Parks. In the 1960s, African Americans were fighting against racism and **discrimination**. This fight for equal treatment was known as the civil rights movement. Parks was a leader in the civil rights movement. She helped change laws that were unfair to African Americans.

Rosa Parks and the Bus Boycott

The day was long and hard for Rosa Parks.
When work was done, she rode a bus
  toward home.
The bus was split in two: the back for blacks,
the front was saved for whites alone.

The bus filled up with people leaving work,
so many whites in front they
  could not fit.
The driver told Rosa
  she had to move
and give up her
  seat for a white
  man to sit.

But Rosa, tired of racist rules, said, "No."
She would not go. Police took her to jail.
The battles then followed for civil rights.
The people struggled but did not fail.

And this we know: one woman made
a difference we remember still.
We'll sing of Rosa Parks and all the folks
who led the fight for equal rights. We will!

?

What features make this poem a ballad?

NOW IT'S YOUR TURN!

Narrative poetry can be about big subjects, such
as heroes and wars. It can also be about everyday
things. Try to think of a story in your life. Now tell it
in a narrative poem!

TIPS FOR YOUNG POETS

1. Read three narrative poems. Think about which ones you like best and why.

2. Make lists of rhyming words. Start with easy words like *cat* and *bat*.

3. Make an outline before you start writing a narrative poem. Write down your characters and setting. Then plan out the beginning, middle, and end.

4. Practice reading your poems out loud in front of an audience.

5. Choose a story from your own life. It could be a funny story or an exciting story. Write it in a paragraph or two. Then turn it into a poem using lines, rhythm, and rhymes.

6. Choose a fairytale and write the story as a narrative poem.

7. Think of somebody who is a hero or heroine to you. Try writing a story about that person.

8. Ask a friend to give you a character, setting, and problem the character has to solve. Use your friend's suggestions to write a narrative poem.

GLOSSARY

characters (KAR-ik-turz): Characters are the people or animals in a poem or story. Choose your characters before starting a narrative poem.

discrimination (dis-krim-i-NAY-shuhn): Treating people unfairly because of their race, age, gender, or another characteristic is discrimination. Rosa Parks fought against discrimination during the civil rights movement.

plot (PLAHT): A story's plot is made up of the events that happen in the story. Every plot has a beginning, middle, and end.

rhyme (RIME): Words that rhyme have the same ending sound. The words *flower* and *power* rhyme.

rhythm (RITH-uhm): Rhythm is a repeating pattern of sounds in poetry. Poetic rhythm is called meter.

stanzas (STAN-zuhz): Stanzas are groups of two or more lines in a poem. Most ballads are broken into stanzas that are four lines long.

stressed (STREST): A word or syllable is stressed when it is said a bit louder than another word or syllable. The pattern of stressed and unstressed sounds decides a poem's rhythm.

syllables (SIL-uh-buhlz): Syllables are units of sounds in a word. You can tell how many syllables are in a word by clapping your hands as you say the word.

TO LEARN MORE

BOOKS

Cross, Gillian. *The Odyssey*. Somerville, MA: Candlewick Press, 2012.

Florian, Douglas. *Shiver Me Timbers! Pirate Poems & Paintings*. New York: Beach Land Books, 2012.

Macken, JoAnn Early. *Read, Recite, and Write Narrative Poems (Poet's Workshop)*. New York: Crabtree Publishing, 2014.

ON THE WEB

Visit our Web site for lots of links about narrative poems:
www.childsworld.com/links

Note to Parents, Teachers, and Librarians: We routinely check our Web links to make sure they're safe, active sites—so encourage your readers to check them out!

INDEX